Sing, Lost Soul

Sing, Lost Soul

Karl Coppock

WIPF & STOCK · Eugene, Oregon

SING, LOST SOUL

Wipf & Stock
An Imprint of Wipf and Stock Publishers
199 W. 8th Ave., Suite 3
Eugene, OR 97401

www.wipfandstock.com

PAPERBACK ISBN: 978-1-5326-3319-5
HARDCOVER ISBN: 978-1-5326-3321-8
EBOOK ISBN: 978-1-5326-3320-1

Manufactured in the U.S.A.   JUNE 14, 2017

For Abigail

Contents

Section 3. Memory

Section 4. Fantasy

Epilogue

Prologue

1.

I read a poem today that halfway in
called me to say, almost out loud,
Now that's a poem!

It was only after half my mind was jogged
and memory stirred that not a week ago
I'd read this poem and shrugged.

Some poems are lovers for all seasons,
some for just a few,
and some, apparently, are one-night stands.

Section 1. Humanity

2.

City summer nights
the smell of tracks
of tar and wood
sparks
L clacks

Food
with smells exotic
and if honest
odd

Strangers could
almost
be friends
if words were offered

3.

The vanity of fear:
the world is bent
toward me.

4.

How came you, little beast, to be so feared, reviled?
Do death and darkness truly harken to your call?
Are you their foreguide or their footman?
Prophet of the endless night?

Or is it color—Is black so obvious?
So ominous? So clear a copy of the dying light?
Are we so simple to surmise the equation of a raven
to the night?

Or is there truth in superstitions that would so catechize
our ready-to-be frightened minds
to gasp suspiciously
at ebon, fluttered flight?

5.

From a wounded side released,
out of a body crushed,
a free flowing of blood.

Come, will you not hasten to his side?
Attend this mass of flesh, this wreck,
this carnage?
Not if it is black?

Wracked by grief, such as I am,
yet I will shake my body free, for mine,
the aching and the numbing both betray, my body

yet has life. Though his does not.
And this, this body crushed, this blood demanded,
this disincarnation, this
I must attend.

6.

Perhaps we'll bring about
our own extinction
silence will pervade

No human ears to hear
the crashing waters poisoned
falling poisoned tree

The earth our raped but virgin
mother bereaved
will mourn and weep

And seventy times seven
weeks of weeks will sit
in retching grief

Till she'll arise
at last renewed, and pregnant
of her own accord

A new and vibrant child bear
then children
and their children in full bloom

Will build, imbibe
indwell and not destroy
their new Jerusalem

7.

The sun, it lingers long to set;
without a sense of urgency, it warms,
and lets its warming dissipate—
so slow to wane.

What have we?
What have we become?
And those we love—how long?
How long since we have known?

This goodness lingering, will it forever hold?
Or will it droop and dim, all spent?
Good Lord!—
how come we to such debt?

8.

I've bruised the day;
it's time to turn
the light and bid this one
goodnight;
tomorrow may
be bold and true and pass
unharmed by my contusive guile
—but not today.

9.

Then came the rain,
wet as ever—
rain, save for delay, will never change.

We wash, we rinse, we dry.
We wet, we shake, we hope to change,
we die.

Like ocean, yet unlike.
Like sunlight, if without a shine.
Life taking, both, and ever sighing.

How, then, rain?—
Are we so other than the stuff
of which we're made?

10.

Unaware
and you become—
breathe,
let slip your mind,
gaze,
behold the world twirl.
You smile and live.

Watching you,
unaware that you are you,
I too become.

Lost at last,
from time to time,
beyond the all-consuming
sense of self,
I live—
in turning out,
in watching something else.

11.

That sort of playfulness
like a puppy
mixed with the semi-self-aware glee
of an innocent almost-adolescent
is purity incarnate,
wine inebriated
on its own rich ferment.

Section 2. Intimacy

12.

Next to me in sheets
so close your soul
gets in my eyes

13.

Where do you come from in the darkness
when you slip in close beside me,
fleeting flutter then gone again?
Where do you go when you are gone?

Can a woman haunt you when you know her?
When she loves you, when you love her?
When she's alive and all around you,
phantom first and then a bulwark?

Where do you go when you are gone?

14.

From the moment you, companion,
stopped me, stranger,
you began to take, and you have taken
things I knew not dwelled in my possession;
gladly, now they cannot be reclaimed
or be retaken.

15.

Hardwood floors
not glossy
scratched and squeaky
pale
not quite the color you'd've chosen
yet somehow perfect
in their ability
to make apartment
home

16.

You're there, I'm here (again).
You're sweating
on a humid Midwest afternoon
visiting our friends.

You call to say you're headed
for a shower then a nap.
And here at work, here at my desk,
I close my eyes and see the image of your back.

The soft curve of your side,
your knees tucked up toward your chin,
I wish that I could cuddle in
and doze a while with you.

I'm fine alone, you know.
I think. I write. I walk. And yet,
I feel a little distant when you're gone:
from you, and from myself, and from the world.

17.

In your not-smile
an afterglow
remains

And in the simmer
in the slide from full to half
to full release
I watch a theme

An arc of anger
doubt, despair
disdain
of roiling life, of letting go

Then you refind your smile,
and both our worlds
are changed

18.

How I told you
you had hurt me
and you heard—
now that is rare.

19.

Soon love I'll be coming
coming o'er the hill
o'er the ripe horizon
soon I will I will

Soon is e'er before us
soon is coming child
soon is ever wanting
soon is our denial

Soon we'll run together
on the open field
blinding bright horizon
hands our only shields

So ever keep your watching
strained toward that hill
soon we'll run together
soon we will we will

20.

We once stood upon a plot of land,
simple, gracious, green,
gladsome, and serene—
that place was not this place,
this place is not our home.

You said we'd not long hold,
and I believed,
but, oh!—
how quick the land beneath our feet!

'Cross prairies of the ever-rising west,
your face while we have trekked—
which gleams from day to day its own rare gold,
whose eyes, which memory hold
(visions, but no less true),
reflect the sun, the clouds,
the intermittent blue—
not once upon my world has set,
holds hope, if now a hope subdued.

21.

Sing
lost soul
the way back home
is marked by falling boundaries
your song will etch and echo, and eternity
will sing, and stones once set and
hardened will to dust
and cease
to be

Section 3. Memory

22.

Turtles
waves
and raves about the sun
the sky
the island by

Surrendered tenderness
of night
black water deep 'neath treading feet
still I'm a child
still running wild

Fire
built for a chance
not for romance
my brother and I

The tug of moon
the ghost of loon
wide-eyed star lust, I must
those waters tread again

I am a child
I am

23.

Hello nostalgia,

I'm not one to linger long,
but you arrive and I'd be foolish

not to listen:
your words are pictures,
movements inner,

and you emerge
from traffic like a holy ghost out of a tail pipe,
winged and unperturbed.
You are here now, suddenly:

I see a picture window,
clear as air
but hung between a child and me,
and I see woods and water like an arc
enwrapping doubt.

Without a doubt, from this I started.
Why are souls, I ask, like water
pouring out alongside water?
—but you are gone,

nor could you ever answer
questions such as these;
I'll seek for meaning elsewhere;

you were only ever laughter,
foolish as a child,

a jester.

24.

This is my childhood,
a summer day,
clouds belie its promise,
on a lake.

This day may warm,
or as it is may breathe,
exhale, and die.
That is its mystery—

it will forever,
without deceit,
intoxicate.

25.

All the old things
ancient in their place
stone
or heavy as
in photos framed

Like whispers
beckoning
like horsehairs
touched
upon a string

Tugs
those workhorses
of weary waters strain
to draw
what's riding deep
in heavy harbor
out of memory

26.

When cold rains come in summer,
our winter clothes all packed away,
what are we to do but stand, our hands
pressed up against the window,
surrendered to the shiver?

27.

The recoil
through my hand and shoulder
through my eye
changed my perspective of the land.

The bird was not a bird
the rabbit not a rabbit
they were other things
and part of other things.

The rocky hills and sage
stood ageless as
and up against
the sky.

The sunlight
pale water to my eye
and I the hunter part
in only fractured ways.

I had not seen
before the kick and call
it all came after
sight was altered,

though sight it had not been at all
'til it was altered.

28.

I have dreamed
and I have set my dreams to paper
but they will not tether there,
they change and flee.

To know most surely is to know,
to set down once for all most surely is to conquer,
but knowledge alters,
and for the life of me I cannot pin it down.

29.

I wish that you could close your eyes
and read this poem.
I closed them as I wrote—
I felt the fog horn blow,

was hearkened back to that great sea,
sweet sea. I wish that you could feel
within my soul—
I felt the tremor as I wrote,

I sensed the thrill, awoke.
Oh, wake, awake,
O soul,
begin to know.

30.

Give me joy
amid the tumble of occluding mist,
between the bruises down the path of knowledge;
slipping, falling, I know this:
that I am glad for all of it.

31.

As a child, I was always outside barefoot,
when it wasn't winter.
For this I was often chastised—
not by family or those who knew me,
but by strangers.

I never understood this, and to this day,
here remains my question, Stranger:
Why shouldn't a child go barefoot?
Even if his feet are permanently stained?
Why not feel the world beneath your feet?
Isn't all ground holy?

Section 4. Fantasy

32.

Having settled some years back,
when the sidewalk was still cracked,
before the young man fell and sued and won,
and the City paid, and paid again
for jackhammers and shovels and concrete
and the arms and guts of strong young men
and strong old men to man it all,
a little seed, long silent, decided it was time,
and growing up in just a three-day weekend,
burst upon the world, and cracked and ruined
everything again.

33.

Between the streambed and the streetcar, muck and zeal, a child,
aware as he may be, goes steady on his way. There is no line.
He steps each stone and rides each rail without a thought
for whether here or there the riffraff are more riffy or more raffy,
wise or sane.

He lifts his head when he is hungry, happy; not when he's distract
by thoughts or wrappers or by flies that sit on windows—
flies don't watch outside. The boy, a-face the window,
sometimes sees what's there upon (hi, fly!) or what's beyond,
what's rushing by.

These lines, the ones within his care, are made to draw him out,
to take him first to what? And then to whom? To where? Sweet child,
these lines are made forever, not for gapping nor for spacing nor for fear.
How can I learn to draw within your lines
that are not there?

34.

Jutting out
peninsular
on either side of Aerie Lake,
the canine teeth of a giant terror,
which had scooped the world—
the lake and trees
and we in our canoe—
into its mouth, and there sat slack-jawed,
waiting, patient till it should choose
to quench its thirst and hunger
in one great gulp.

The world
in the monster's foggy breath
hung silent. And the terror that so held us?
It held silent, too. We watched, and nothing moved.
No sound but gravelly growls,
water on the shore.
The monster, so it seemed,
would wait a while.
We passed an eerie day upon the lake
inside the monster's mouth, not knowing when
we would be swallowed.

35.

Prowls the fish monger
with his eyes,
his thin supply is eel—
too like,
too many years spent
side by side.

The hunger gnaw is real, the craving,
and the cavish space beneath the soggy drape,
his hiding place.
Emerge, withdraw, emerge, withdraw.
Do what your eels could not—
escape.

The world is strange
beyond the awning dank,
too bright the clouds, too strong
the tug of human want.
Emerge, withdraw, emerge,
withdraw.

36.

The bones of trees,
quiet on a line of sight.

They neither spoke
nor bent beneath the wind,
they stood
straight and strong;
or scattered, stretched, they rested
on a meadow, alpine, fair.

They did not speak
and yet they spoke as graveyards speak,
and they instructed me
about the grace of dying.

37.

When the shadow became neither a friend nor an enemy,
but a common passing stranger,
common such that we could share a nod out on the street,
I knew that I was safe:
that my breath could rise and fall more freely in my chest,
that my smile could rest more deeply in my head.
Shadow is a neighbor, sometimes sad, but always true, and common.

38.

A bold surrender
took him in his later years
to places he had never dreamed,
as from his stubborn pitch
he gently eased,
adventures waiting
like a cooling
and invigorating stream.

39.

Emerging from a crumbled roof, a stony wall, a tree,
green on gray and red and brown,
like a gentle and unhurried sprout,
arising from a soulless thing that once was called a house,
a shell, now cracked, decrepit and discarded,
useless, but to give an also once discarded seed a garden.

And why should trees not grow from houses?
Why should stones once stacked and guarded
not eventually fall outward?
Plant themselves within the dirt
in which they once so deeply and unhurriedly hardened?
Should not a flower in a graveyard blossom?

For much is cracked and much decayed, and much has fallen,
but all was always meant to grow into a garden.

40.

deeper now
sleeper still somehow

what beauty
unabashed by daylight

differentiating not
the moon and midnight

splitting not the hairs
of lived and lived right

41.

She woke up on a field of flowers,
not down among them, full on top, buoyed,
the hills and gentle-bowing stems asway,
rolling, waving like the ocean in its ebbing, flowing way;

But not azure, aqua, emerald green,
her ocean was a blazing fire
of yellow and orange and red
and all the vibrant colors in between.

Just how those flowers held her there I could not say,
but Jesus-like she did not sink,
and as the ocean mirrors back the sky
hers mirrored back the blazing sun,
and whether closed or open wide
her eyes, smiling, dancing, burned with holy fire,
and yellow and orange and red and happiness were one.

Epilogue

42.

The ground beneath
my feet,
my kingdom

Here I stand,
unshaken,
irrevocably me

And all are welcome

www.ingramcontent.com/pod-product-compliance
Lightning Source LLC
Chambersburg PA
CBHW062033040426
42447CB00010B/2268